SWIVELMOUNT

SWIVELMOUNT
KEN BABSTOCK

COACH HOUSE BOOKS, TORONTO

first edition

Published with the generous assistance of the Canada Council for the Arts and the Ontario Arts Council. Coach House Books also acknowledges the support of the Government of Canada through the Canada Book Fund and the Government of Ontario through the Ontario Book Publishing Tax Credit.

LIBRARY AND ARCHIVES CANADA CATALOGUING IN PUBLICATION

Title: Swivelmount / Ken Babstock.
Names: Babstock, Ken, 1970- author.
Description: Poems.
Identifiers: Canadiana (print) 20200295152 | Canadiana (ebook) 20200295179 | ISBN 9781552454138 (softcover) | ISBN 9781770566491 (EPUB) | ISBN 9781770566507 (PDF)
Classification: LCC PS8553.A245 S95 2020 | DDC C811/.54—dc23

Swivelmount is available as an ebook: ISBN 978 1 77056 649 1 (EPUB), ISBN 978 1 77056 650 7 (PDF)

Purchase of the print version of this book entitles you to a free digital copy. To claim your ebook of this title, please email sales@chbooks.com with proof of purchase. (Coach House Books reserves the right to terminate the free digital download offer at any time.)

For Helen, who is everywhere in these lines,
and for our young men, Samuel and Luca, everywhere in our lives.

Nature is the wheel
When you get off the wheel you're looking out
You stand with your back to the turmoil
You never rest with nature, it's a hungry thing
Every animal that you meet is hungry
Not that I don't believe in eating
but I just want to make the distinction between
art and eating

—Agnes Martin

When it's there it's there and when it's not it's not and basta.
—Samuel Beckett

Contents

Self-Portrait, 1864 Self-Portrait, 1896 Self-Portrait

I started dragging Cézanne
on Twitter—the bot posting
canvasses, no discernible order—

about a year back, on his
birthday, which is my birthday,
making us each as earthy, as

stubborn, practical, not given
to extravagance, self-reliant,
detached, unfussed by material

goods, prone to morbidity,
patient to the point of inertia,
unmothered, emotionally

avoidant, driven to infer meaning
from context, overly fond
of a sardine and whites

from the sandy Languedoc,
anarcho-syndicalist by nature
though homebodies in the event

of actual rioting, affronted
by whiffs of the transcendental,
afraid of dentists, sexually

omnivorous, fiscally infantile,
unready to renounce
psychoanalysis in toto

while alternatives remain
limited to CBT night classes
and homework, disinclined

to afford benefit of the doubt,
doubtful of benefit, slow to open,
open to indolence, solicitous

of others' esteem in private,
private, piratical in the aesthetic
realm, domestically recursive,

allergic to church, interruptions,
and gambling, devoid
of long-term episodic memory

rendering sense of the self
chained to the present
tense, gun-shy, importunate

in pubs, hyperpareidolic,
ornery, saturnine, vengeful,
glum, and given to huffing

the turps as the other, being
capricorns. Though here's
a thing, we're *on the cusp*

of aquarius, Paul and me.
You know what that means.
Everything to play for! An open

concern in the late nineties:
immediacy as a poetic practice
might be a reification

of the status quo, as in, hey,
friend, I can hold your compact
mirror while you touch up,

sing to you from behind your
ovoid reflection, if it's all the same
to you? I have a screen grab

from spring showing *Rocks At
Fontainebleau* squeezed between
Roma's De Rossi screaming

at Samp and Sontag's diary
from 4/6/49 below:
'Nothing but humiliation and

degradation at the thought of
physical relations with a man.'
Why did you ever go near

the human form, Paul? I mean,
your bathers are atrocious,
atrocious in your eyes

even as you painted
their buttocks and lumpy torsos
as turnipy, waxen, over-leavened

pains de campagne, arranged
their intimacy to exclude
you, us, leaving them talking

and damp against the damp
grass and river rock
in cool evening shadow pinks.

They pass by periodically now
along with Hortense, a few
black suits, men in a bar,

a boy in a loincloth, not one
of them fully convincing.
Perhaps you wanted release

from the mountain's chronic
dissembling, the unfinished
trees and outcroppings

pounding their dumb note
of mass and relation. Perhaps
you were lonely and knew

of no working ameliorative.
Perhaps you were lonely
in the face of stone and bough.

Good that a supportive
community has formed now,
though, so many subject-slices

you couldn't have known
in the south, and Sontag again,
'Last night I said in my drugged

post-migraine sleep, "I hate
your mind."' By which I believe
she meant the very weather

framing the horse chestnuts
west of Marseille was
the phasing of catastrophe

in and out of your filtering
front brain, set up *en plein air*
three-legged and fingertips

made of horse hair. Do we
find ourselves wanting to spit
the chewed pigment over our

hands again held over our
heads as the captured do? Crocus
midwinter the very cave wall

and canvas and standard
of a crushed comprehension—
Another death after the farewell

to an idea of a charnel house
we live inside as sentry, nurse,
busker, and tenant. You

had me at tree but I've lost
me again, back in a tide pool
totting the money in a pinned

crab's purse, the chest plate
folded back on the four or
six discs as the hydraulic

peel grab of six legs detached
from a jib leave their impress,
weaken, twitch, and let go.

Abject, a cancer would say.
Little fan-and-bubble drama.
Little expiration of walking

rock; the mountain never
returns whole from having
been worshipped to pieces.

Edge

A stone-saw's circular
      blade is diamond
tipped.
A pneumatic drill's
      bit is carbon alloy
with a hexagonal
fit.
      The oxygen ions
in corundum
form a close-packed
      hexagonal lattice,
tough,
abrasive, amphoteric,
      aloxite holds
fracked rock
fracked once
      the water's drained.
It gives
sandpaper its grit,
      is the divot
of chalk
powdering a pool
      cue's tip.
The six,
a kiss, in the side
      pocket. Consider
the atom;
if there's a way
      of breaking down
a thing we'll find
a way to break it.

Tasked with Designing the Vienna House

After a wet spring, the rattan mat
that spent May caught in a maple
looks like hair, a note of horror
on a cul-de-sac, blowing out kinks
under lamplight. The modest row
of semi-detached homes pull
their blinds at my tower block
making a good show of being
put upon, poor things, their
petunias. Sky of bright rust and
soapy aquamarine. A half lemon
wrinkles, extrudes slick seeds,
and the flies appear. I don't know
how I do it. How the city does it,
constantly appearing as paper,

collaged and aswim in emulsion,
then tipping over into dystopia,
white cell count of the expressway,
the cellophane chill, the organic
chicken. I love graffiti for being
a constant among the variables.
Least aware when I need milk
for the morning, the unplanned
script is everywhere its own fiat
and mark of lives asking I licence
some unseen assembly. In one
version of living a non-viable midlife
under the present aesthetic, I'm
to *reach people*, I take it, my laser
pointer, my pager, though the last

I saw of them they waved happily
from a quayside bar in Rotterdam,
glad to know I was away safe, or
away, and would damage no more
of de Kooning's mom's hotel.
Europe's like that, awash in names
and hard drugs. In Rotterdam I sat
in a very narrow folding seat while
Tranströmer played 'Piano Concerto
for the Left Hand' which Ravel
had written for Wittgenstein's brother
who'd lost his right hand in the war.
A vessel bursts in my right eye.
A vessel leaves port bound for my
right eye. Imagine the right feelings.

Aubade from Security

Again at St. Pancras, across from the Crick Institute's
thoughts writ large, making up its façade while
we keep something back, for next time. Dissipated

day-moon glimpsed at Blackfriars over Russian
glass before the sun slams in, the Montaigne swims,
and I'm dabbing my cheek like an otter. The Den, your

gran's old haunt through the twenties, orthogonal,
manichean shadows now carving the empty east
stand into spectral home and away blocks behaving

themselves, singing nothing, silent as East Croydon's
concrete in the messed-up weather. 'Let me know when
you're through security.' Then a fence of Xs. Arms up,

sock feet, all I am or own bathed in backscatter X-ray.
You get swabbed from my hands by a wand and blue latex.

Homeoteleuton

Reading Berger doesn't
help one to draw, so
one rereads Berger
that it might help
one to draw,
to unstitch habitual

sight and bed down
with cattle, and with
fowl, and with the ass,
as with landing NASA
probes, the hard sell,
or greeting new dogs,

so much is riding on
the approach—what
has ever held one's
regard, ever?—sponging
up light on a stool *en
plein air*, cracking

Klee's online Bauhaus
notes on colour and line,
rigging an adjustable
perspective box
like the one in Vincent's
notebook but from

Meccano, MDF, mint
floss in an X, gestural,

expressive, prosthetic
extensions, red grease
pencil on skylight's
blue glass. For a year,

as it died, I did my
iPhone 4s in graphite
on heavy white stock
meant, I thought, for
watercolour work, then
I'd photograph the weak

rendering (black irregular
polygon quarried from
the obelisk in 2001),
bent over it in sunlight
trying to add something
with layers of shadow.

I called it not drawing
with no light, once, then
never again, *per cola
et commata*, as description
worsened so went
the symptoms, in fact,

the vanishing point
failed to appear outside
the textbook, whether
the inner model goes
in for strict mimesis
or is only locally functional,

the figure in the tower
crane's cab must still
come to ground for lunch,
all angles and planes dis-
arranged by a life between
luff jib and transient load.

Category Mistake
for Anna Politkovskaya

She was told no. She would not stop.
She was told no. She still would not stop.
You see what dynamics are in play—
three times is for children, junkies, dogs.
These cufflinks, guess what is inlaid
in their gold beds. You can't. To catalogue
immiseration in fine detail's a fine life's
work, for some, and decently paid.

Her obligation was to her kids. Their grief,
inscribed on her headstone, is all history
needs to know of her. If that. She died
knowing the risks—or didn't, and just died.
When the horse rears up, I eat pellets of sky.
When the horse of state rears up, I eat.

Another American Massacre

Then   I brought them to where it had happened and showed it
to them.   It was sufficient and not at all sufficient that the ground
had been   marked ahead of time. A line scored in the road a fair
distance shy   of its location. Yellow tape. A guyline anchored
in soft ground   adjacent with neon buoys tugging in what wind
there still was. I   pointed to demographics, zoning laws, founding

documents, patterns   of investiture, exceptional circumstance
and -ism. I pointed out   the obvious, then drew attention to the not
obvious. I was standing   alone to one side (neither alone nor
off to one side) in functional   field gear. I asked for ID, affiliation,
clearing each mute observer's   presence with those above me
and with the necessary laterally   aligned organizations. I stood

proximal to it, so had for myself sensory   evidence of it having
happened. As did they, I presumed. I stood   proximal to it though
no closer to it or not close to it in any sense   that mattered, as I
commonly saw non-white bodies when and if   they were not alive
and not here and not legitimized by virtue of. I   saw them finished.
Commonly. Which became the signal for my own   work to begin its
levelling trip toward a sea, an absolute sea, of work   identical to it.

Fiat Nox

Fox down the spine of Kantstrasse. Mitternachtsfuchs.
                    A non-thought travelling Kant Street. I won't

be leaving this to itself. It would require no more of him
                    in clarity of judgement across a range

of possibles than it would of his witness and pivot
                    to alter his emerging moment

at the level of percept—*just turn away*—such that likeness
                    to any other thing with extension in space

meets its cancellation on the tongue.
                    He has a tongue, it's just a different tongue.

Gas fume and hatmaker's offcut.
                    Third rail in a power surge. Jacobean stoat.

Christmas sock in Pirate City. Kanadische Kunstlerinnen,
                    IT start-ups, and minstrelsy on the National stage.

Torched sedans beneath Airbnb lofts
                    smoke Swedes out of Mitte, adding

a page to the burgeoning grimoire.
                    They even burned Quentin's Beemer, the glorious

Scheisskerle. Russian machetes turn melons
                    to stoplights outside Charlottenburg S-bahn.

So he heads not in that direction. Wisdom.
                A set of instincts that accrue over time. I lived

in the flat next door to a flat Jarmusch lived
                next door to Arvo Pärt in, if you follow.

We should by now know what's wrong—
                it's not asking much to have built by now a critique—

It's within reason to expect by now a median clarity—
                Kantstr. to Museumsinsel's rats and white swans.

Imagine the livery. If I could ride him I'd ride
                him north to the east sea then west to the north

sea then south to the west sea then east
                to the south sea.

Millstone and Cistern

West of Leslie Spit, west of weekend birders
strolling the access road tuned to grim news
from the sandbar willow and trembling aspen,

lake-liners lower the great tubs of themselves
into narrower tubs of rust water and blue oil,
cut from the portlands re-gen, below

cement silos and defunct soy storage. Bright stars
in a diesel cloud, ecstatic vision some muskrat's
subsumed in, as dead grass, plaited under the new

growth, emits a papery, dehydrated prologue
to the wet *glunk* signalling a body swallowed
by ideation. Was it the oughts we spent giving

wood ticks all the airtime? Dislodged by mutating
flus, mutating viruses, the dread mutability
microscopic and eyeless. Magnified millionfold

they could displace the paisley and geometrics
that so tire us, fractal and grid, dihedral symmetry,
pareidolia and apophenia all the days of our

lives. I read the script in the twisted rebar, refer
to my map of vowels in the mouth, and feel, suddenly,
for the dredgeate, material forced to relocate by

the barge load. What are our sympathies for, if not
the unseen contaminated, the unnamed tonnage.
Whole tech sectors born on the city's gluey silt.

Husbandry in N4

Dendritic splay of pollarded planes in winter
make a brain of Hanley Road. Dreams go,
then come again in altered dress, changed

names, new topologies, and narrative mess.
You tell me what they mean, as palliative.
It helps us live, the blister pack of conjectural

talk. The sky's a hard graphite. Carbon monoxide
resides in the planes' bark—it'll scab off, love.
A communist sets out stalls on Stroud Green Road.

No one moves, though, from the Old Dairy. Our
boys, with their mom and their dad, would not
easily know us. Canker stain, anthracnose, lacebug,

and frost cracking the cracking bark. Ungava gin
and Ting. We'll represent ourselves: fodder, fence-
posts, baskets, boats. Pruning cycles determine

a landscape's use and shape, as temperance or
game theory or any habit grows to resemble a drug.

A Bracelet

To raise and look at one's own hand in dream
        is to break, they
say, from the mis-scaled maps of dreams—
        so one hand gone,
not there, in some sense should serve to join
        whole part to not-
other, invert internal worlds so being in
        one is identical
to engulfing another. Inside, it holds a hilt
        that isn't there,
draws one arrow from its quiver.
        The toy-sized ball
hitch on the stopper's chain went in its socket
        then wouldn't come
out again, or I believed, when I was small.
        But one gets taught
some links are for shorter, deeper terms,
        some a single ring, like
this bracelet is itself, itself the edge of things.

Puma Dalglish Silver

Coal miner Sam Bartram, scouted by Charlton, played
keeper for that club for the next two decades. Christmas Day,
1937, Charlton met Chelsea at Stamford Bridge in a fog
so thick swaths of the stands stood empty by half-time
and players were colliding like trains all over the sopping
pitch. Bartram, late in the second half, patrolled his area
like a shark in shallows, peering into an off-white miasma
where his outfield players had presumably pinned Chelsea
back. Sam listened for an oncoming counter-attack, the hot
snorts and boot-squelch and barked orders, but the fog
kept mum and thickened, the uprights pulled on pinafores,
the chalked touchlines became blank hoardings that piled
up and merged. From out of the stew one dark silhouette
approached at the wrong speed, walking, and swinging
a stick. 'What in bloody hell you doing here? The game's
been done a quarter hour, mate. You've won.' Which was
good news to Sam, on paper, though it didn't feel right.

Monarch Park

Park grounds and sky a gnawed bone, grey white.
Or the snow dirties slightly, transitioning

to a featureless overcast. Black galleons, bare
maples at anchor. The black forms are human,

left to right and right to left across the blank
drifts and into depressed trails, pulling sleds

into which they've deposited one child or children.
The people moving, the people moving and

hauling their young behind them in humped silhouette
appear to disturb solidity, the fixity of dumb elements

arrayed in the scene, deposited there as dark
stroke, gestural mark with mass and heft. Hibachis

on posts, slatted benches, a fence dividing nothing
or decorating the sour linen in diamond shadow lace.

Single cinderblock structure, its windows
shuttered and exterior cage bulb unlit. One dog

rubbing its own face in it all. All told, perhaps a third
of what's visible is dark form, opacity punched out

of the white that constitutes backdrop or medium
our gallery of physical law has seen fit to force

being into, fists and fissures of matter unhooked
from their home, set stirring across a toneless

panel. It happens to birds likewise, dark-eyed juncos,
oily cowbirds, evolved from volcanic rock, forced

to double back into the arrangement having found
the frame to be limit in the slurry of western sky.

Forgive our pinched field of vision. Forgive our position
as outwitted witness, having slept so deep we'd perish

were lines not to converge in the froth of distance.

Peak Spader

Discreetly the undersea cables make landfall
at stations south of Lunenburg, again on the coast
of the Carolinas, again at Widemouth Bay
where Apollo , TAT-8, TAT-14, and Yellow (AC2)
are whisked away. Not a night goes by deep-water
sharks aren't at the polyethylene sheathing
along some juncture of SEA-WE-ME 3. We love
the light for its polluting effects. Love how unseen
we remain stood undressed in his field of vision.
Not a night goes by. We feel graced to absorb
what lumens are there stood undressed in the eye
of the luminous flux. Redstarts go headlong
into the high structures, their brief lives a ripple
in the tuned sloshing damper above and we
honour each by waking to more light, our star
in the sixth of its seven-year cycle, blanching and casting
about for admirers. A voice that could make
crêpe de chine in eau-de-Nil come. We remain
nameless in photographic memory but he gets
a little hard at the sight of past injury. A falling
man in the shadow of the wings on the tarmac.
A form falling through the vertical wind shear.
His voice burnt and slowed to hypnosis, he
could sell you things, or end us, terminal desire
being its own beauty. Powers of sight concluding
just off the coast of the patrician face. Bend at the
waist in wasted light working late in the urban core.
The move from satellite to fibre optics increases both
volume and heart rate by orders of. Received wisdom
said Light The Place Up, and it was lit up, and desire

found new space to see itself perform. If we could
all bunk off class at Andover and have Jackie serve
us supper. If the day were anything less than saturated
blue illusion, anything more. Breathless at her neck
in the moment she succumbed. They come ashore
at Bude and the white radomes suck them up.
The predators are after the sheathing or they're
after the light inside, we can't know as they operate
deep in dark fathoms—a night goes by in a pulse. Pause
to reconcile the farm labour with the binge watch,
the special dentistry with the democratic urge.
He loves us in pink. So swath the earth in it. Rituals
declare themselves for the Anthropocene's thirteenth
pontifex, behold the disarranged grid of eaters
in the extreme white of the food court, eyes like
sheep-face stunned at the core of the Fuller Brooch.
Soon we'll ask a generation conceived in light
what it is to be conceived of light, their original
dark contraband, illuminate sin in a dish. No ground
from which to claim No Strings. No dark inward,
no Scapa Flow, ignorant inlet inside which entire
fleets scuttled in a night's welding bee. We are all
accountable in the wind farms after the art party.
To fit three in a Corvette coupe, best the third be dead.
Flower and Stone show him they own Stone and Flower.
A wall gets built. The chariots rise, the chariots do rise.

Chloros

> 'My Life, your light green eyes
> Have lit on me with joy.'
> —James Merrill

Event, word, news, aggregator, new news—
waking distraught, we climb through hoops
of pale sweat toward bed. None the wiser.
Cropped photo of a broadcast of a mass,

a system, a concentric darkening, one relation
among relations accompanied by a graph.
Well and good. The screen his hand sweeps
over, indicating effects will be continental

in scope, is green. In scope. We imagine
a pallid green, the shade behind what
presents as allegory. The spill, spilling over

the system of borders, like those delimit
what is imperative we see. They're in gold,
floating above ground, where time slows.

I Am No Pilot, Yet

It resembled a city insofar as the streets' scales blistered,
projecting emergency's tricolour over façades, upturned
fruit boxes, ivory gowns, and the gurning skaters who heft
their broadswords among the flock of screams bouncing
between bank towers. We say, when we must, 'the small
hours' to indicate dimensions such that nothing much
could have happened within them. They were simply
too small. We forgo saying 'consequence,' we'll pass
through that anyway, just as we pass through nights into
a newly illuminated balcony scene, a Japanese maple's

shade turning the gazpacho the shade of Japanese maple.
Or city has nothing to do with the poem, and it's not
me on foot headed west believing west to be exactly south.
The sky changed, in the interval, black tea to congealed
grease—here it comes, the subjective—with strips of darker
vapour marshalling energies in the distance. Let's just
say the sky changed. That intervals went unlogged.
I know for certain I thought I'd been of the opinion I'd
left the apartment in boots. When I have my hair cut
I am materially different. When I forgot someone entirely
I was indifferent—immaterially. The front edge of tomorrow's
weather might be this yellow doughnut-light tired people
so often start yelling in, despite the sprinkles. If I eat my father's
watch off my own wrist, can the stars' not being there stand
as hard evidence of insect divinity? Can thaw not mean thaw?

Dream of the Cerne Abbas Giant

Facing the stern of an alloy canoe—
        adrift with a signal—I was crushing
my son, FIFA 15, Spurs v Dortmund,
as he and I slid
past petroglyphs,

past pictographs, Jenny Holzer bits, unlikely
        gang tags too high on the rock
cliffs. He'd pleaded leniency, injury
time, that I relent
on the Gegenpress

but I felt emboldened now, driven,
        vindicated by the weird rise
of rough water and two-goal
cushion, a chop
summoned by no

gale but a pulse on the steel drum of our hull,
        our boat auto-piloting
shallows, shelves, explosives
of deadheads, and
years out of sight

from where we put in or kicked off. The white
        heart line double-hitched to a steel
bow plate dragged on the surface,
I noticed, like lost
graphite figures

trawling for whitefish. All thumbs now, I bossed
          midfield because I could, my Castro
keeping his Dembele to heel, my Piszczek
always where his
Dele was not yet.

Off starboard, out over the black serrated
          tree line, our night sky split its seam,
horking up luminescent medieval green
fungal light, and a red
braiding through

from a pierced central wound. That display
          told the time, which we took in stride,
mostly, but for his dipping one claw
in the cold wrinkled
lake, once-removed

moonraker, chasing not the white Artemisian
          crown but this primary-tone
procession of burst blisters, gasoline
wheels spidering
black water,

praehistoriae speculum, um … Leaving his paddle
          to bridge the gunnels, he raised
himself to his full height in the wonky
boat. 4–1 in the eighty-seventh
minute when he spoke

up for himself with a conviction, an unfamiliar
          deep note verging on tenor. He

wanted, he said, to not be the age that he
in fact was, wanted
to no longer be

even the he that he was and couldn't not be,
        inexplicably snagged in the cross-
currents of now and here. He used 'unfair'
to describe his
allotment as he

saw it. 'That dark wall over there'—timber line,
        I corrected—'that dark wall over
there is my opposite and putative enemy,
a permanent,
impenetrable

redoubt. I am a stick thing. Chalked-out and
        ditch shallow, brute contour without
mass or perspective. I cannot see even what
might be approaching
from below or beneath.'

All ribs as he said this, all ribs, spear, and dick,
        all cowlicks and a green world visible
beyond him. A shrinkage of empire, an un-
naming of islands,
protectorates,

colonies, commonweal held to be whatever
        we commoners hold it to be.
As point of emphasis, he now threw a dab
the size of a highway
grader and the boat

rocked. 'When I self-stim you're not locked
      out so much as reduced, I spell
can cast spells—Trismegistic—all spokes
meeting their hub,
Thoth in a tub

with a maker looking, looking, in his bid for
      a doubled self.'

after Börje Salming

And what is it to be transfixed
as a child, in love, already
modelling or building a schematic,
a feigned world beyond one's world
of Essex County's Bible-edged

sunsets, spring swamps, and canola.
That centrifugal glide—little brother
of wild Stig and a Sami father dead
in a mine—in your Jofa lid, pewter
bracelet, and Daoust blades

I could neither source nor say,
that stride and elegance Kiruna
had raised then thrown
to the xenophobic wolves of Philly,
Boston, Buffalo, us. Our King.

My love now lifts the disinterred
skull of an unnamed grunt whose
face was split in half, 1461,
in the snow at Towton and talks us
through the carnage, that's Börje's

face, the face I carry and wear
under my own as armour
in a campaign of losing and losses.
'28,000 dead in a day.'
206 stitches and back on the ice

after three days. 'Two claimants
to the crown and no quarter given.'
Backbone of the 'Tre Kronor'
whose half-visor and hyper-awareness
I longed for from within my face-cage.

Sun dogs over the soft ice of a rink
in Tecumseh. Over Mortimer's Cross.
To Dave Hodge on our Panavision
I said I'd hoped one day for a scar
like that, so my father kicked

my head at the curved screen.
There was blood on the ice, a blue
to the blazer and the leaf
blazoned onto the freezing white
river.

Bonavista

No point thinking I could do it here, either—
though I love the barrens, the wildflower and lichens
where the trail runs out under a decommissioned
lighthouse. You don't see seals in the swell, it's decades
since they came into the knowledge people live here,

in a paucity of trained doctors and rental cars,
a standing promise of the coming of oil, turn
in the economy, return of the fisheries, an internship
in tech or wind. Caribou racks get nailed to a tuckamore.
The terns have their notions, seen fleeing over

breakers, nicking the horizon with dark blades
from under dark hoods, ornery little flight simulators
levelling up and never getting nauseous.
Speaking of, what's the distinction between pot
to piss in and plot to piss on? One buries one's father.

The Sea at L'Estaque

Because the slip between blue
and battleship avoids the crosshairs—

the crossed branches that knock
in a wind some distance inland, too

weak to hold the bucket of sunlight
spilled at the hill's crest, too weak

or too flexible, naked, tapered, true
to their own work, and shortsighted,

which together is a kind of strength—
the mind lifts the wall of sea, hauls

it nearer the village, a stalled, looming
storm wave, its own display case,

the glass in a dark aquarium visitors
want to pass through unharmed

into a deranged new propulsion, breathe
differently, grab hold of the boneless

slick skin like palming an eyeball,
live happily in the depressurized

element, thoughtless amongst kin
with no north or surface or death

to speak of, to internalize as cardinal point
or lodestar, etched deep into the so-called

future. A log, say, a segment of ship's
mast, rotating as though on a drugged

lathe, takes the long, galvanized nail
to a depth of one inch. A second nail

driven the same depth in the dense wood
adjacent, a third abuts that, a fourth, so on,

continuously, as the log continues its axial
roll until an undulant metal fan of spikes

skirts the log's length. On each flat
nailhead is fixed a machined filament,

a powerful light, wired one to the next,
so a circuit of sub-zero blue saturates

the surrounding air, its multitudes
and granular impurities, rich smoke,

sleek carbons, innocent, residual, ancient
cells the poets sing of and name dust.

Deep nimbus of woad or Egyptian,
as related to tapeworms as it is to TV,

to diving wrecks as it is to distance,
it refuses to speak or blink and turns

in its chamber without base or support,
without reason or lifespan or use.

Die Zwitscher-Maschine

I watch the blue
birds emerge from

snow, in real
time, successive,

identical but
for each one's

variant theme or
range of temper,

wistful, baleful,
indolent, vindictive.

They stay their brief
moments, leave

a syntax of prints
I might worry for

meaning if I weren't
called away. Cheap

speed by post, a client
in silks, the Voynich

manuscript, and
Durex past their

due. I've lost my
mid-weight copper

wire, so the present
lies unbuilt, unused.

Which of us now
inhales the city

as though mock
orange were in bloom.

My burner, my
balaclava. What a

notion, honestly,
what a notion

Meditation

after Baudelaire

Another pink one, Sadness. It'll take the edge off.
You begged for dark, dark's here now.
Toronto's under infected quilts, beginning to cough,
the gilded few quarantined, the rest of us cowed.

Our dying polis come up in purpuric welts
at all this choice, these niche markets, lifestyle's whip
ending at 5 AM bent over American Standard; cults
of the last rail, Sorrow. I'll chop it up

before they come. Drip drip. The dead years
gag in knockoff labels from a nineteenth-floor terrace.
You can smile like a ferret but you're blind, submerged.

A bled-out sun face down in the underpass.
Non-night, in its ferraiolo or gas cape back from two tours
—gurgling, pleural, O Love, listen— arrives as an urge.

Milk and Hair

Buffalo south over the marbling lake seen
pitching an errant new mall. Clear mornings

I'm meant to be comfortable with the American
vernacular, it was meant to happen between channels.

Stop pretending you can just up and start thinking—
it's mostly snooker, sardines over ham, the sense

of having pointed to Door Number 3
at the business end of some steamy

ruminations. At ease nowhere in the murk
of Rathmines, the gaffer hid me behind a ventilator

hood while union reps inspected the worksite. Illegal
labour stashing pay packets in a heatless Georgian squat.

Equanimity in the face of aggression such
a virtue among flowers of the meadow, the rest

of us should *express ourselves*—'One
eye sees, the other feels' said Klee, and Andromeda

there in the feed being gold leaf on cake trailing
coordinates. Space, right? Then ghetto spider. Kid can

dance. Presence shuts the lid of its music box. To refer
to oneself in Bremen one points to an egg. If you

manage to tear it clean from its spindle, clingfilm
does what it's told, keeping the dead alive

that little bit longer. Yes, I've gone camping …
Am I coming across as a man speaking? I'm not

proud of it, the silk underlayers, the sharkskin
Dintex soft-shell Tactical hoodie. At least I

refrain from song before a fire. This year, to
choose between the Barbed Wire Museum

in Kansas and the Goderich Salt Mine, I'm
throwing a garden spade at a targeted ad,

spending my miles on what mammals hold
in common: debt, nerves, milk and hair.

Beached Squid and Ideas of Order

A singer born with a sound in her head
lives to get it out. Looking down at the balsamic
pooled on a plate she sort of *is* the eye of the squid,
is the vinyl-black disc on porcelain, the physics

lesson, and the fable of deserting one element
for its opposite. So she tests a note against the shingle,
earth's percussion always lonely for an instrument
as abraded, contingent, orphaned, and intermingled

as itself. Music can come from a carcass if you're close
in and finger its hooked beak nestled in the drapery
of the arms' suckers lined with chitin, the two tentacles
retractile like a second, shredded mantle. *A priori*

a singer could live to her own end and never get it out,
the sound, itself a late addition and not, in fact, innate.

False Ecology

Lamplighter. She'd built a candle-powered convection heater
from graduated terracotta pots, bolt clamps, a bread

pan, and beach pebble spacers. I lived in dread
of ever being cold. Thus the layers, the windcheater.

Keeper

Having been bit while offering water to a rabid dog, Emily Brontë took herself to the kitchen in her family home, removed an iron from the hearth, and cauterized the punctures herself, being so thorough as to singe the white of her own ulna. The prospect of unduly worrying her family being anathema to Emily, she said nothing of the injury, enduring the subsequent infection (though not of rabies) and revealing the events only once she was again healthy enough to tend to animals.

Patrick, father of the Brontë sisters, endured 'with extraordinary patience and firmness,' eye surgery needed to remove a cataract—the entire lens of the left eye being extracted to avoid recurrence. Belladonna, a virulent toxin, had been applied to dilate the pupil though no other measures that might reduce discomfort in the seventy-year-old, who sat 'without flinching or complaint' and later made notes on the experience in his copy of *Modern Domestic Medicine*, were given him.

Emily's loyal bullmastiff, Keeper, was once caught muddying white bedding after having been warned off previously. Emily dragged Keeper downstairs, punching him repeatedly into submission. Later, nursing his swollen eyes, she let him know there would 'be no hard feelings.' When Emily died of tuberculosis, the mastiff 'followed her funeral to the vault,' 'leading the procession to the cemetery,' then into the church, 'lying ... at [their] feet while the burial service was being read.'

One villager remembered Keeper as a 'conglomerate, combining every species of English caninity from the turnspit to the sheepdog, with a strain of Haworth originality superadded.' This may have been one of the villagers who stood in audience as Keeper fought viciously with another large local dog. Emily inserted herself between the two, throwing pepper into their faces and pulling Keeper off his victim by the scruff. Neither dog nor owner was known to mix with other humans by choice.

Emily completed, as she had with all family pets, competent sketches of Keeper sleeping by the fire, where she'd regularly lean against his bulk as against a chair back, reading for hours. It was during these evenings, absorbing Keeper's heat, Emily reported to be in the real presence of both sisters who'd died before even her eldest sibling was born, and where she'd become convinced a metaphysic, rather than any material course of events, gave rise to the spectrum, visible in its entire, from greens at the wood to blackened lip.

Traplines

Confucian thought's packing them in at Harvard again,
notes the *Guardian*, outdone
in enrollment only by 'Intro to Comp Sci'
and 'Intro to Econ,' holding steady at number one. By

these measures we'll have a first cohort of selfless (we do
mean selfless) straphangers on two-
tiered Google luxury buses
evacuating the Castro of a morning, making lifestyle choices

none of us could have seen coming. Not one of us
might have foretold
the four-fold
increase in crafting among the buy-less demographic. Plus,

the chip implant for the 'correction' of deafness
is not only hackable
but likely already hacked, a dirigible
on magnetic rails from Kuala Lumpur to Inverness

isn't beyond the bounds of the thinkable now, now
that our boy Confucius is, like Affleck
says through flecks
of Schlitz, *wicked smahwt*. We might back down

from imponderables and be judged prudent (Rorty?
Aurelius?) but having crossed the Rubicon
of forty,
it's not like we'll be found in 'Intro to Econ'

hatching plans to 'collect it all,' mine each deep
packet, monetize the attentional dream sleep
of the next cohort grabbing fixer-uppers
in Eureka Valley, like trappers

inheriting their forefather's mink line or profitable line
in mink—
One dynasty's line of code, we could say, is another's line
in 'Königsblau' Rohrer & Klingner fountain-pen ink.

Milk and Hair: A Translation

Upstate New York's up to its usual shit, I suppose,
though I can't see it from here, unlike my shoes.

If you find that compelling, I have hash I can sell you.
You keep saying you know what you want, that you

arrived here after a series of difficult choices, that
you're not one to be fucked with or disrespected.

I've been where you are and turns out I didn't and am.
Don't ask about the goat in Howth. Or Miss Havisham.

Wildflowers are cool enough, it's just they're
not of much use, being neither purple or

delicate. I stare at shit on the phone and am amazed.
Then get sick to my stomach at having eaten nothing.

'I have two words for you: Plastics.' One word. What?
Yes, I have slept in the 'Canadian Wilderness.' It

is like the nightmare where you'd kill for a place
to shit while everyone's screaming through their face,

pointing out patches of poison oak. Help yourself.
Here on in I stick with my kind. Sectile bricks

to crumble and spin up, eyeballs going deep-set, priced
out of the city along with the florists and choice dealers.

Precious Ally

The damp outer leaves of street cabbage
kicked up by a blinkered dray horse.
Miniature manila pay-packets, cement

dust in the electric kettle, blood sausage,
and the three-speed pushed around
Ranelagh and Rathmines, depending,

having gone over its handlebars
on O'Connell Bridge, for the tourists.
Skin infections I healed myself, autophagist,

in a Gardiner St squat with borrowed iodine
and a carpet knife. Innocent garblings of
Dún Laoghaire, Drogheda, Baile Àtha Cliath,

and Fiànna Fáil. Paul McGrath. Ooh.
Ah. Scoring outside the Pembroke
Hotel on the eve of Thatcher's fall—

the tears. USAF refuelling at Shannon.
So many asking was I Czech or East
German or Ulster, as though reticence

while blasted might indicate History.
Stashed in a rooftop air-con vent
as union reps harried the gaffer;

flat-capped extras from something Irish
at the Abbey by Behan or O'Casey.
So young. I first heard 'The Mercy Seat'

in a vodka paralysis beneath Clodagh,
who, being older, didn't seem to mind,
or did, and I couldn't see for her thighs.

Casino barge on the shadowed Liffey.
Wine bars habituated by gangsters and U2,
where a bottle of champs meant a month's rent,

solicitors bigging up flats blooming like
mushrooms on the Barrow and Suir.
Sent round the sites for forty feet of shoreline.

Being asked to sing. Being urged by strangers
to sing out loud as the room goes quiet. Hells
Angels pounding the tables with stubbies—

Hexi Telly

Lampfire, Fuelghost, when will I see you again?

What is it you see when you look?

Bipedal form in contour, poppy fields.
Night-vision graffiti greening the walls. A Chinook.

Any flame like mine, then, would do.
Any blue.

In the Brecon Beacons, before being badged, I emptied
my life into—

I've four hours remaining. The scattering's
a stand-in.
It happens above you.

I remember the scattering, the trying to blend in.

These pictures you conjure while looking,
they're strange?

Strange if human-on-human is strange. I held up a head.

Like a lantern, as in Dante.

Like an apple or torch, as in Goya. I was a boy, once.

That is gone. That's all gone.
What's left?

Interrogation. Pattern. False gods. Endurance. Fraternity.

So take me with you into the desert
of civility.

The Plural of Unconscious, or Painting the Forth Bridge

Single example in the OED of its use
                being owned, at least,
by a volitional subject, is Norman
                Mailer, of all people, havering,
'but that may be my
unconsciouses speaking.'

Living ten flights up, the sky's traffic
                comes to displace street
level stuff, the raptors, bush planes,
                passenger jets,
pigeons, and orange fire
balls NE to SW over Scarborough.

They activate the canvas's upper third,
                enviably chalky northern
light rinses the middle strip, and children's
                screams, deprived as they are
of transitional objects, buoy up
the base from down here.

We've learned in the past, haven't we,
                to mark how
usage warps held belief. Warped
                or mistaken usage bakes
belief into the user as raisins
into despicable loaves

of malt bread. Unchecked, we're eyeing the Bedouin
                in the cassoulet. Tying flogged

friars to a bull's rack before salting the tinker's
                         dray horse. Chiellini, not
Keano, has the face of a condottiere;
Roy's is that of a galloglass, as a friend

put it, in her keynote at Caius College. Who doesn't
                         enjoy putting Alan fucking
Bennett in his place? Lemons weigh
                         green on lemon trees between
Monterosso and Riomaggiore. Olives
in ground nets. The Via dell'Amore

taken by landslide in 2011—small losses.
                         You may feel, in your infinite
jump glitch, time is on your side
                         but have a look at Rod Stewart
now. Where are the faces who tore
at our youth as hawks

into possum? Not vacationing
                         on the Bosporus, I'd wager.
My brother contracted scabies, leaving the
                         ringworm to me. Shocked
twin chimps opening green
hymnals until service let out.

The green bled out. Gram stains
                         ID'ing what type of cells
we'd be, or become whatever pathogenetic
                         later strain. May all
Christendom remember them.
And genuflect, as Beck might do

— 68 —

at the loss of even one plectrum
               from the shark's smile
biting into the chrome of a mic stand.
               You may think I meant Jeff.
I didn't. No one did. The strobes
and engrams have an effect.

', comma,'

after Graham Foust

No nasturtiums slung
from the screw hooks.
A squirrel runs
the tension wire
to a transistor coil,
all coiled tension,
sophistry, self-talk.
Evening midges
doing senility above
the water main.
Waterline on concrete
from last year's floods.
Let's be mindful. No,
not like that, as needs
be. The overcast,
you'll notice,
brushed an expensive
Himalayan salt,
infrastructure
dating to the year
I was born. This fire
hydrant and a hostage
crisis. Concorde's
first flight, the floppy
disk, Isle of Wight.
I nudge the swivel
tap and clean water
appears, depress
the doohickey,

my waste removed.
The first smart phone
was a Rubik's cube,
the first Rubik's cube
a snuff box, the first
snuff box likely bone
beading. The comfort
in knowing one knows
what one knows
without asking much
of oneself Hegel
called ordinary. I like
to sit down in my
ordinary, bothering
no one, unchanged
by the unchanged
object, totting up
the times I stayed
out of it. It's conceivable,
or it should be, that
a decade of Vaseline,
station wagons, rayon,
and combs might
have shown me
a window in which
I gifted myself the end
of myself, and it endured
up to now, that gift.

And Mars Passed Close to the Sun

I'm writing this in a hurry, bringing
its two ends
        together to keep

the oil from the water, closing
it in on itself then watching
it wriggle. I'm
        hoping to pip her

at the ribbon, before her own bomb
drops in the next number of *Nature*.
It's been forever, or less,
they've claimed an
        archaea host—

we're in terribly close now,
the mitochondrial rafts
in the single cell's Sargasso,
way way back at the business
end of geological
        time, life's first

murk or sea-vent event or
pure accident—
must have cooked its own materials,
whatever ingredients needed
for interior membrane walls.
'Must have,'
        'somehow,' always more

god where the gaps come from.
Eff that, she'd thought, back in '01
and chased a hunch the alphaproteobacteria
had their mitts in the game
in heretofore unseen ways. Those ways
are known now. She knows them.
She has footage:

                  jittery, luminous,

smeary drip moving from earliest A
to A-1, or exactly home in a dark
the colour of migraines and horological
seizures, who knows, but without
signal or fanfare this Lite-Brite gloop
up and *sheds a vesicle*, pinches off
a piece or packet of itself, herniates
a bladder of

                sub-self that detaches,

becomes a probe or Trojan gift bag
of lipids, iron, and recipes for iron
and I lost my grip on it then, in
the lobby of the Royal York, where her
diagrammed napkin of blobs within
blobs helped none at all and even
her lipids colleague leaned on Edenic
metaphors as pedagogical tool over
dirty martinis

                and male scientists

in herds surrounding the cell of three
thought them lab techs or just here with
me, biochemistry is a social sphere as much
as anything is, half its time spent
fending off physics and other zealots all
to prove life began shedding vesicles
and may end over soup in Zurich, Santiago,
or Houston, haemorrhaging thought
bubbles with plans for Baja after
presenting the team's
                    paper in *Nature*.

Filler Sonnet

If one eye sees and the other feels, a barrier
runs between the two kinds of input. Contour

remains left; tone, intensity, and for instance
yearling cubs unsteady under a snow cornice

fall to the right with Beethoven, the Buzzcocks,
parts of one's past. When I knew the two cheques

would cover only rent, I cut back, hung out a shingle,
and lost weight demagnetizing vhs tape. One angle

on events, they're neither current nor coherent,
though loss of them would bring about boredom:

grey screen, room tone, just us and the houseplants
unfurling into the stillness of a negated palatinate.

There was a thing here, initially, I was leading up to,
not hinged jaw or spring, the singing of the swivel chain.

Alonso on Carra

I liked Carra the most he is
The biggest Scouser in the world
We got on well from day
One I think he realized
That I loved football
And he loves football too
We would watch games together
And talk about it every day
I think he respected
That I would enter
Arguments with him
He was always very loud
You could hear his voice
Above everyone else's
I would say 'Carra,
Shut the fuck up!
You have no idea.'
He liked all of that
The confrontation
By 'biggest Scouser in the world'
I am not meaning anything
It was Carra I liked the most
I told him I considered
Tackling a sign of having
Made an earlier mistake
He hit me that day
It was snowing and people
In Liverpool waved
And honked their horns
Rafa said my mandate

Was to feed Gerrard
Now Pep calls me a funnel
Carra would understand
None of this and all of this
Carra, you must understand,
Came to Anfield from Carra Sr
My duty is to be risk averse
I punch my left palm
And say 'Shape. Shape. Shape.'
When Bolton won a free
Kick during my debut
The army from the defence
Moved forward and
The ground began to shake
It is not a straight line, Carra.

Clotho, Lachesis, Atropos

Not normally drawn to the pre-ordained
        but in Max Liebermann's
The Flax Barn at Laren his weavers
retreat, freed from their
wheels, hand-turned

by children on stools. Pearly North Sea light
        traces tangents of flax-
thread warming the women's hands.
The barn could revolve
around one central

post, a parallax effect reducing the weavers
        to few, partially block some,
while children remain shadowed lumps
at labour, engines
in wooden shoes

none of us can not see though don't bother
        naming. Each should be
mounted on *Strand Esel* in lee of coastal
dunes, sea grasses,
sand fleas, and

the tufted manes. There's a photo of Walter
        Benjamin, age four, perched
on a beach-donkey at a Trassenheide resort.
Short pants, his little knees,
his gaze hooked

on a flash of bright beyond the left shoulder
        of the lens that's trained
on him, though I would say that—perhaps
to him, he's looking exactly
where he's been directed

to look, smile, please, hold the reins and wait.
        Overhead stage of a pier
follows perspective lines, dutifully collapsing
at a roofed shelter some
way out to sea,

low tide, the vertical and offset piles climbed
        by kelp and mussel reverse
the light-dark schema of the donkey's
legs or continue Walter's
bare, plump legs

disappearing into black ankle boots. Weirdly,
        if you look for the photo
online it comes always twinned with one
of Kafka at six, in studio,
holding the reins

of a toy horse-slash-sheep, deeply aware of his
        ears in light, ferns, fake
spruce staged on broad planks arranged to mean
wilderness keep company
with his thick wool

breeches over black knee socks and riding boots
        we can count the buttons
of. The sheep-horse has a feather in its cap,

a single hieroglyphic
eye. The young are

to die when we say in service of our need
            for replications of them.
I've kept 106 digital images of Jack and Rosie,
the animals my son
would not ride

that summer at the Scarborough seaside.
            Infinitely gentle, blanketed
donkeys with eyes like misted bitumen,
he'd stare, from a ways
off, then slowly shake

his head, even walked the same circuit some
            distance from them as kids
lined up for their turn. Where do they live, Dad?
Who named them? When?
Don't they get bored?

He didn't ask me any of that. Not then. And has
            no memory now of ever
having been there, the crab's shell drilled
through by gulls I showed
him, the turn in weather,

far out over water, as though the sea had risen
            in anger. The walk back,
all quiet, holding a featureless stone striped
once by quartz, common,
but his now, kept warm.

Feeding Pod

Thirty or forty in grey zeppelins of capelin. A wait
staff of puffins panicking beyond the waves' swing door.
Back to this again—the abject smearing into the sublime—
in Witless Bay no less, a washed, murmurous, silvery
erotics mooning close to the humpback's exposed,
dilatory blowhole just off our bow. Freud said something
salutary in the brochure about a keyhole but it's this
we should maybe not be witnessing having already
paid to do so. The reel burbling over the catamaran's
PA, black metal mesh on the mic head, the telephoto
lenses, are all Natural. Streaking murres, our
attention spans, are overstretched, can't light, settle,
or choose one direction of travel, so I won't come
back to this again, bottleneck at intake, those foil pinwheels,
cascade of coins in the fountain's basin, the callow
disregard of black ducks far out on the frozen Volga.
I reconstruct remembering the young soviet's eyes as
limpid, bored, duotang blue beneath red stars. Red star.
What I've come to take pleasure in should be hived off
from calamitous boredom and serious endeavour.
The wind one mile up isn't the wind we're panning for grit
down here at shop-window level. Let Visa give your
friends the credit they deserve, we'll raise our sons
on mung beans, on Minecraft, and Leopardi. They'll be
sad, but forever carry an appreciation for the grid.
Was it Giacomo or Pasolini with the ankylosing spondylitis?—
If he did, at least he could not then have known he did.
SatNav's barking northwest to the flipper pie, so just drive.
The dorsal fins of bulls get dented by bigger cows riding

roughshod. He said that? That, and something about
napping briefly on the surface, half one's brain awake,
forever crying for nothing. This one rolls and throws shade.

In Medias Res

Like David's Marat swanning
    a little too whitely

over the lip of his tub,
    the lip curls gallicly,

pouting tiger lily, as the steam
    leaves, last wisps,

asps of breath he tries
    sucking back in defiance

of the utensil so recently sticking
    out of him. And what

is it about his head? Right—
    cropped close, a shower

cap? Is a quill drifting loose
    from his fist? A thought

is a hard thing to hold, even in
    a mouth as open as—

FaceTime

We've either been garrulous
long enough
or, like those aquaculturists who've chosen
to farm estuarine waters
while monitoring both temperature
and salinity,
sheltering a Broodstock in simulated
conditions as the vibrio
risk moves to within controllable range, yet
and still produce
a harvest each whatever, we now request
from each other a moment
to swallow what's been said
before it's chewed
a week, or found to host a slickly polished
nubbin, an endosymbiotic
commensal guest,
a delicacy itself,
adding layer to meaning, nuance to content,
a sidewise thrill and gist
never given a chance
to stretch its legs having lived to now
in the ruched, plicated dark.

Three Skulls on a Patterned Carpet

We shine at these blunt recycled
mornings, vinegar on the brush
bristles, astringence, self-denial,

the light's hymnal or scorpion finds
me mumbling to an associate,
in our cell, on our terms, making

our outsider art—though in
the minds of the churlish, our
knowing the term should exclude

us. Let them exclude us. We touch
our common parts, naming
as we go: sternum, lobe, eczema,

crotch, imagining life on a beach,
paddling this side of the buoy
line, the young with their pails

and their fat divers' watches,
the cloisonné of the far Labrador
shore someone's catafalque

through ice crystal and low fog.
Dried capelin that smell of hibiscus
and mown grass, nitroglycerin,

deer spray, and penance.
Tuesdays we hang from a hook
he set into the ceiling beam,

dangle and sing, crosshatched by
window grate shadow. Our ribcaged
nightmares offset the pleurisy,

the inhalations, the raspy laughter
at the harvest moon. He found
me here on my own, back before

everyone's long-liner converted to
crabbing and commodities futures
was a thing. 'We need not be real,'

he'd said, 'neither of us. No one's
forcing the blood round our circuit.'
I told him I'd never been strong

on narrative structure. 'You won't need
that here,' he assured me, 'no event
can arise between two cancellations;

it's like putting Time up for winter
in jars with the rabbit and jams.
Trust me, you're no longer named or

believed. The reverb's turned way up.'

By Lacustrine We Meant No Luck at All

It spoke—that child's rendering of the Thin White Duke—
and sipped from a schooner of cold milk while raising
a banner that blocked out the sun. Behind each staging
of warm apricot, a colour theory derived from Goethe's
original, itself deeply flawed, leaving us to enjoy evenings
predicated on water striders, ignorance, and deer flies.
Not one among us inclined to say sunset, so we run the shore-
line, read from bills of lading, the lyric ballads, the belles
lettres: O burin and copper plate, O reel-to-reel, though donkeys
be intuitive, social beasts, they carry within them the load-
bearing centuries of steep labour and fine war. Refined
war. Just as the peppered moth darkened in adaptation
to atmospheric black carbon, so too can our bay porpoise
open a can of Pepsi by whistling a phrase in Farsi. The river,
its found level in lowlands, might widen its lips in the cresses,
the mosses, the skinks and striders of the carboniferous,
the drill holes of bank swallows encoding the mud—Herodotus,
giardia, and amygdalin—legal briefs, biblical surface fires,
softening bill of the eared grebe. Coke levels not thinning
fish but making the fish more thin. Osterberg in a Berlin
car park being driven by Jones into abutments and sheet pile
walls. The rushes encroach, the fresh water recedes. Lac de Manque.
Ankle-deep in dead water and razor clam, voices carry for miles.

Power and Privilege

Not to wet the sand under
your capacity to know your own mind
or point to solar flares
at the appearance of the rainbow ball,
but are you sure you're all right
being in love with me
because I'm not all that functional
or wise or anything?
Closest I've come to watching
Night of the Hunter was reading
an account of Lana Turner pissing
on Robert Mitchum. I've only
just begun banking online. No one
ever includes the freeze response
alongside the other two autonomic
ones. Like biopics of writers,
it's low in action,
drool not being big box office.
I didn't go to school, anywhere,
never mind Stanford.

I think, no, I worry (it's worrying)
you fell in love without
necessarily inspecting
all of these questions. I know I'd be best
served by talking myself somewhere,
like Christoper Robin, somewhere
a friend lived—lives—within their means,
stuck in their own doorframe, or expecting
diminishment as more of their lot.

They spent the pages together, didn't they,
obeying the narrative, jumping
in with a quip now and then if the weather
got up, or one of their crew
peeled off into their particular obsessions
giving everyone else something to mull
over. Has Disney bled into
my earliest—? We've all had that nail
through the sole breach the flesh, then
endured the tales of typhus, the dear
old diphtheria, one or the other

going by its street name stood over the drain-
grate kicking at the buckling tarmac.
My brother said cocaine can give you lockjaw.
Like the rest of the world's bits,
people either connect or they don't, it isn't
for me to intercede or force the issue,
and look, the chimney pots of Sarajevo
are the city offering the assembled mountains
endless cigarettes at dawn.
I burned ants as a boy. The sun can be narrowed
to a blade. Still, the patriarch
in the Melrose novels
applying the red end of a cigar
made me vomit. It's in the telling, isn't it?
We locate power on a low
stone wall under a fig tree.
We do it all day every day until we can't see.
We do it with a belt between our teeth.
Did you wake to a world vibrating off key,
sick at the root, pale and untenable?

Domestics as the Origin of Given Names

Pulled out of class early fall I
was told it was urgent at home,
I'd be needed in Greenspond. I
bound books in their strap
and took biscuits and goose fat
for the five-hour trip, arriving
past dark round the back where
my father handle-fed me a spade
and something bundled in pilled
bedcover or burlap. I don't now
remember its weight but the light
from the mud room was yellow and
stopped halfway to our south fence.
I dug the night a tongue in the earth,
ignorant, obedient, though life since
has suggested I did know more than
it seemed while I stepped down on
the blade and levered up stone.
It went in deep. I stood the spade
back in the shed. My sister returned
by train to her domestic work
for a family in Great Falls. Arms
raked raw by raspberry cane,
I slept late in my brother's bed.

Stove in the Atelier

Is torture not implicit
or embedded in
the prevalence of
the superscrapers?
Not their foursquare
embodiment of accum-
ulated capital, silk
trains of dominance

and erotics darkening
the throughways
and depeopled districts—
tiaras of helipads—I
mean their brains of brute,
fluid tonnage held
in reserve as slosh
damper, false moon

dangled as counterweight
to cyclone, sway, and tremors
in the fragile crust. Having

forgotten how to erase
the episodic, one backfills,
backfills with aggregate,
with confected enthusiasm,
a reasonable coming-to-be,
and the mainsails from
model ships having passed
through belief's

bottleneck. That is
a white-throated dipper,
isn't it? Entering the current
like needlepoint,
restarting the stitch
upstream having run
the river bed's gauntlet.
'Displayed,' in heraldry.

The Sugarcubes' B-side
cover, 'Top of the World,'
cued the alternative end

of history in '92, and
the Cremaster Cycle isn't
about you. A train can
be heard wooing a high
trestle some long way
off. There's Woolf's
The Waves and there
are the cycloid and
sinusoidal curves,

superimposed and
graphed, modelled
in software. There's
spaghetti and spaghetti-
fication. Memories from
the feed declare vertical
shear is desire tearing
off the cladding, flaying

the structure. The I-beams are
I-beams, the forms are the forms
of prayer from down here.

Single Cell

If an ass comes to in a holding cell

         midway between late, thin sun
and a daytime moon, between vibrations

         of clock cages and being
concussed, absorbing

         the puce tones of industrial gloss
on the breeze block walls, what impetus

         has he to take the form
either of a bull or a butterfly,

         the bear-in-den or the Slivovitz,
Burin's drowned or the foxfire light?

         Apollo's crimson beeves?
When you arrived lit up you were machine.

         I want to help you—
But I, like other gods coming good

         on lost wagers, doing a stint
among the asphodel, taxi meters, red dirt,

         feigning affinity
for tumbling seas, launderettes surviving

         on dead blocks, and a worked
up furor when plumplings suffocate,

         must first fall between stools
in the silvering realm. You'll know

         then I am present to you by thunder
and by cameras on swivel mounts.

         Neither the ass nor the razor-
wire appears in any extant writings.

         Security tape is a TV trope, like

the threaded glass in the single portal

                        through which you see cyclones,

no, pheromones making wet runs

                        in black nylon. The sun's just a

hate rag, blotting striations of cirrus,

                        cross-sections of a disinterred skull

looking for ground meat or low fruit

                        in the brain's laterality, hair whorls

and handedness, excitability and one

                        gene's on switch. Kinks in the ruts

lining the approach to the road here

                        where to die of hunger is to prove

another's conjecture and be thirsty still.

North Sea Vespers

The smaller boats came into harbour last,
a white plate in each wave crest and the gulls
long quit. Seiners, gillnetters, who knows,
little storm floods attached to what I guess
were the bridge hatches or doors. Coked-up
seasonal men disposing of old cabbage and fat.
I remember the first time I learned E. coli
was contaminating produce as well, not only
meat, lakes, pools, faucets, and phones—

     ... drifted in among the flags and stuck.
People feel compelled to teach you things.
People are mountains. We tried, god knows,
to make a love but the day went on beginning.

Not Not Negative Theology

Use shell shard to extract
          shell shard
from the albumen,
said no one who's ever

read Berryman's *Love
          and Fame*. They
know how it ends.
I did not arrive here

via an account of then.
          I don't trace
causal relations to moss-
faced dolmens in Cornwall

or Navarre or Sylt or
          the Burren, nor to
cold-poured shadow
in some lunar graben

where a swipe at
          parthenogenesis
didn't actually happen,
nor to the embodied

mind kicking or bucking
          when haptens
cling like burrs to the
variorum of sensory

nuggets the abducens nerve
          keeps making us
look at, nor to hallucinogens
like ayahuasca, or

starvation, nor that time
          on the limestone
barrens we brewed tea
from chickweed,

elevating androgen
          to dangerous levels,
earning one of us
the apt cognomen

'The Satyr of Burnt Cape' or
          'The Cape Norman
Goat', the sadder the sea-
bottom the more covered

the abdomen in crabs
          and mites, it seems,
it might seem the fens
of East Anglia watered

William of Norwich's fame
          at eleven but I'd
rather be twelve than tinder
for Christians' fiery

self-fashioning. Solie's been
          mining the cave

walls ten years, mind, her
monks in the drip drip

of their Neolithic dens at
          the Forth's edge
the fjord's edge the Forth's
edge. Amen.

Grip to Ground Connector

Geometry of the indolent, the shirkers,

    the holstered ratchet and Metallica T,

the rigger in cycling gloves, the paid-up member,

    the daily, the skinhead reading García

Márquez, the hungover biochemist hoarding

    three treatments at Mom's, the paroled,

the stargazer, the undercover cop, the capoeira

    brown belt who went down on Jolie,

c-clamp jockeys, the naphthalene moon-wranglers,

    the diabetic gamers, the art historians,

the redeployed craft services chef, the butch

    lesbian boxers, the acned, the hyper,

the wrong-channel merchant, the father of four,

    the speed-dealing Rhodes scholar,

fantasy novelists chewing holes in their cheeks,

    colourists, arborists, entomologists,

the Benedictine novice quoting Jay-Z

over lunch, the orphaned and oversexed,

Trotskyists glaring at cherry tomatoes,

epileptics, onanists, some dude with a recipe

for killer grilled cheese, bipeds, bisexuals,

brown baggers, gymnasts, monarchists,

pedophiles, and originalists. We all just sat there—

one, two stacked, one flat one upended,

three if in truck after wrap—while the films of our

deaths got made under budget.

By Torchlight Through a Ventilation Brick

And do you then see how exploding transformers
express an irregular division of what sky
is still visible? And then, at the blue-white spectrum
end, do you see the lampblack
on metal, shadow on hinge and plate,
the vestigial print of unseen power?

1348 saw an island's inhabitants
reduced by half their number. It would appear
the earth took back every other soul that stood.
Just clawed them back and left a stench.
First to see the folly of the forced march
was a horse of a soldier of the Grande Armée.

MIT saw an opportunity so took it, the computers
kick on, tasking away, ever-doubling,
gunning for the quantum state.
And we see how the shafts fall across lead,
striping the eternal crypts in a Rileyan metaphysic,
discrete and geometric, objects goofily decoupled,

presented axonometrically, smelling
of nasturtium and damp brick.
The lesser Sarah as long and as wide as
the rediscovered patriarch walled off in a wine cellar.
What family demands is rediscovery, or licence
to haunt, deploying a semantic lever

the rest of us live poorly on. A supermodel saw
the forest green of the surface

structure's entrance from her window's window,
the glassine sparkle in piled aggregate, the slack
spring of the rat's body, the divinity's infinite
grudge, wet holly, the blood of cooked intake and sorrow.

Infinite Jump Glitch

Still centre of an expressway overpass, the terrain vague
       of this eastern borough;
the mood rich in mission creep, overcast, Camus's *Plague*
            yellowing on loan.

There remains the glitch, like a jump glitch, of working subject
       into the landscape—
itself an *echt vollständig* description of, not the subject,
           the landscape.

Selected Inventory

A clock, an instrument of measurement,
measures intervals.
Your face an instrument that measures change.
Change measures depletion in the self,
floaters in the visual field,
intervals during which no face appears, the hands
fold one upon the other.

Eureka jump seats, an early form of Uber,
are now repurposed in the carceral state
as ferries and they deliver unto the next world
Arkansas's damaged and innocent alike.

In the mind of a child, instruments
                of torture,
                                the super-colony
                of Argentine ants
numbering in the billions. The child's

mind embodied in the child in her
                house built
                                above the super-
                colony. They pour
from faucets, not in the child's mind,

and continue their march toward
                eternity. There's
                                a subterranean
                hum around dinner
time.

Or we might call the Internet simply
the relations between entities that
would not otherwise relate. A rain
barrel measures the dolorous sky
in litres, say, but shares no language
with the armies of fire amassing at
the town limits. Time is slower at
the top of a six-foot ladder. Between
the rungs are intervals. Measured
by the change of your facial muscle.
Ligature. A single bulb at the fuse end
hung from the eye of a plaster ceiling rose.

Perspective is a tool the Dutch acquired as money flooded
into Rotterdam, nearly breaking the banks of the Maas.
Land was lost. A bridge is a silencer on the muzzle of torsion
and measures nothing. A bank with no gold is a truss.

White phosphorus is a moral light or compass.
                    It can be seen in the eyes of newborns.

A Hurricane is a fighter jet,
    or air-to-ground missile, or
        helicopter gunship fitted with an eye.

Cimex lectularius
prefers to feed
exclusively
on human blood
and serves as an
adhesive to the social

body, allowing us to live
in a sustainably
intensifying
density. The front wings
of angels
are vestigial
and reduced to pad-like
structures.
Translucent
nymphs measure the
quotient of evil
in a city
through choral singing
and the rudimentary
use of tools.

A shark is a tool for testing
the veracity of claims for parthenogenesis.
Great Whites have been observed
off the Cape attempting to eat the sun.
Hammerheads, their own faces.
Greenland sharks are an analogue for unspoken
snags in your emotional geometry
left for years to drift silently under
layers of surface ice. The pressure is incredible.
The sun, also, is incredible.

Brushed-copper Zippo
lighters are what remain
of the chivalric order.
To be hired freelance

is to be asked to smoke
between floors. There
are words worth sharing,
after which we should
not say more. A candle
in the window is a door.

Lightwell

Not a dragon's but my own tooth,
and not even whole, half,
having split
in my mouth then spent
months in a duffel coat,
raked out with loose change
and cigarette foil on a street
in your city;
litter now, weak seed
row. My own phalanx stood at arms.
I'm to toss what in the centre of it
just to keep me intact? You're
on your way back. Crossing
provincial borders. Three of six
bulbs in the lightwell now dark.
The field of battle now dark, and
Thebes in blackout but
for campfires at the gate.
There's a seven-
year truce with the earth, the end
of which sees earth swallow
the sword. Whole.
Which results in no word.
Would you have had one? I mean,
at the ready, knowing
an army could be assembled
so quickly? The self dissolved then
relocated so quickly? I'm never
sure if it's agency
or deep structure that wants

what it wants. From street
level this should appear a strafed
space. Bathed in light.
I won the capital and now it's mine.
To appear kind, I killed,
after you'd come, a funnel
spider then dismantled
its black lily flue. Just
now I'm wary of exuberance
outperforming nature,
tactlessness getting the better
of brute fact. It was your
stone and your serpent and your
stage on which to act.

Wetterhaus

On her seesaw, a kerchiefed woman comes out
into dry air, clean light, high swan-white strips,
while inside he waits for the cat gut
to swell, for drizzle or a downpour to gallop
over windbreak and field, lowering cast
to the cloud pile, slugs blooming on the cowpath
like fungus. Traps and blades could up and rust.
From her separate door she'll re-emerge with
blue breaking through grey. Another thin day,
another spell of keeping her balsa-wood
twin in his unlit room playing skunk or solitaire,
losing weight by not drinking. Dry, he could
be a manageable dream she keeps in a hand-tooled
box. She, the law that regulates his mood.

Velodrome, We're Not Out Yet

but we're going to be.
I like the buzz
through the bottom
lip, on my Garneau,
saying 'velodrome'
whether I'm in one
or not, which
I never am—so then
say 'easement
spiral' for a current
through the tongue's
tip while in a track
stand, then
might sprint past
'superelevation'
to catch residuals
from both while
pretending I've no
brakes, but quads
of bagged cement,
head a frozen tear-
drop suspended
from the dark disc

wheel's mydriatic
stare. A spike of
gravity, cyborg's
axis, reinforcing
pedal clips, saying
'centripetal' out
one side of the mouth.
In Dorset's desert
of '76 I came home
over baked earth
from the Kimmeridge
Ledges and turned
on The Tomorrow
People. Bled inside to
be Tomorrow People
and entrusted with
a jaunting belt. My
happiness has always
needed a screen
onto which its forms
can be cast as ghosts.
Water coughed out
of the faucets silted,
I stared at a cricket
bat. I could hear a girl,

older than me, in the
angular shade of
blistering change huts
under the cliff at
Swanage Beach, crying
in her suit, sandals,
for a future she'd not
yet seen as it circled
a day from prior to
those she'd logged.
Lapping itself now
and coming no
closer to conclusion or
restart or reason. Just
crying, then, as we do
on days when we've
ourselves to be with
at the sea. I could hear
her. She could hear
the Zenith's channel
knob chug over and
forcefully click.

Notes

'Self-Portrait, 1864 Self-Portrait, 1896 Self-Portrait,' is for David O'Meara. This poem, along with 'Millstone and Cistern,' 'The Sea at L'Estaque,' 'Three Skulls on a Patterned Carpet,' and 'Stove in the Atelier' are all titled after paintings by Paul Cezanne.

'Homeoteleuton' is for Eric Boelling. Homeoteleuton is a literary term meaning '[An error in copying caused by] the occurrence of similar endings in two neighbouring words, lines, etc.' (*Shorter Oxford English*).

In 'Fiat Nox' the German *Mitternachtsfuchs* is my best attempt at 'midnight fox.'

Several of the lines in 'Peak Spader' track the career of James Spader over the course of his film roles.

'Dream of the Cerne Abbas Giant' is for my son, Samuel Babstock.

'21' was commissioned by the Toronto community newspaper *The West End Pheonix*. Börje Salming wore the number on his jersey throughout his career with the Maple Leafs.

'*Die Zwitscher-Maschine*' is titled after the painting by Paul Klee.

'And Mars Passed Close to the Sun' is for Professor Heidi McBride who holds the Canada Research Chair in Mitochondrial Cell Biology at McGill University. And can drink you under the table.

'Not Not Negative Theology' is not for Karen Solie. She would neither agree with, understand, nor like the poem. So it isn't for her. No way.

Acknowledgements

Many of these poems appeared first in the following journals and magazines. I'm grateful to the editors of each, and to everyone giving time and labour in the world of print publishing. *Granta* ('Power and Privilege,' 'Peak Spader,' 'Tasked with Designing the Vienna House'), *New York Review of Books* ('Edge'), *Oversound* ('Velodrome, We're Not Out Yet'), *POETRY* ('The Sea at L'Estaque,' 'Grip to Ground Connector'), *Magma* ('Infinite Jump Glitch'), *Poetry Birmingham* ('Meditation,' 'Hexi Telly,' 'False Ecology'), *The Scores* (',', comma,' 'Bonavista,' 'Lightwell'), *Michigan Quarterly Review* ('Category Mistake,' 'By Lacustrine We Meant No Luck at All'), *Brick: A Literary Journal* ('Self-Portrait, 1864 Self-Portrait, 1896 Self-Portrait'), *The Manchester Review* ('The Plural of Unconscious,' 'By Torchlight Through a Ventilation Brick,' 'And Mars Passed Close to the Sun'), *The Fiddlehead* ('Filler Sonnet'), *The Well Review* ('FaceTime,' 'In Medias Res'), *The South Dakota Review* ('Selected Inventory,' 'Monarch Park,' 'Aubade From Security,' 'Stove in the Atelier'), *The Rialto* ('Feeding Pod'), *Ambit* ('Husbandry in N4'), *NUVO* ('Three Skulls on a Patterned Carpet'), *West End Phoenix* ('21'), *The Walrus* ('Clotho, Lachesis, Atropos'), *Conduit* ('Fiat Nox'), *The Honest Ulsterman* ('Dream of the Cerne Abbas Giant,' 'North Sea Vespers'), *KLIMAAKSJON* ('Milk and Hair,' 'Milk and Hair: A Translation').

For invaluable support over the past six years, I wish to express deep gratitude to the Canada Council for the Arts, the Ontario Arts Council, the Toronto Arts Council, and the Writers' Trust.

Alana Wilcox is a publisher like no other. I do not know how she does what she does and I'm proud to call her a friend. Alana, Crystal Sikma, James Lindsay, and everyone at Coach House are incredible. Thank you.

Matt Tierney, who edited this book for the press, is not only, it turns out, a brilliant poet but a frighteningly engaged, and engaging, mind. I'm very grateful he gave nothing a free pass.

For decades of love, friendship, art, conversation, poems, and laughter, David O'Meara and Karen Solie, it would seem, are stuck with me. Declan Ryan, Kevin Connolly, Eric Boelling, Will Burns and Nina Hervé, Andrew Zawacki, Gil Adamson, Michael Helm, Michael Redhill, Barb Panter, Dan Bejar, Marisa Gallemit, Jim Bryson, Michael Winter, and Heidi McBride have all shown up at important moments, making those moments more important.

Luca Ferraro and my son, Samuel Babstock; you two are wonderful. Thank you for putting up with your writer parents. For causing the poems to start up again, and then offering them their first ear, Helen Castor, all love and gratitude.

Ken Babstock won Canada's inaugural Latner Writers' Trust Poetry Prize in 2014 for a body of work in mid-career. His fourth collection, *Methodist Hatchet* (Anansi, 2011), won the Griffin Prize for Excellence in Poetry. His previous collections include *Mean* (1999), winner of the Atlantic Poetry Prize and the Milton Acorn People's Poetry Award, *Days into Flatspin* (2001), winner of a K. M. Hunter Award, *Airstream Land Yacht* (2006), winner of the Trillium Book Award for Poetry, and *On Malice*, written while in Berlin as one of DAAD's International Artist Residents and published in 2014 by Coach House Books to wide critical acclaim. His poems have been anthologized in Canada, the UK, the US, and Ireland, and translated into Dutch, German, Serbo-Croatian, Czech, and French. Ken Babstock was born in Newfoundland and lives in Toronto with his son.

Typeset in Arno and Gotham

Printed at the Coach House on bpNichol Lane in Toronto, Ontario, on Zephyr Antique Laid paper, which was manufactured, acid-free, in Saint-Jérôme, Quebec, from second-growth forests. This book was printed with vegetable-based ink on a 1973 Heidelberg KORD offset litho press. Its pages were folded on a Baumfolder, gathered by hand, bound on a Sulby Auto-Minabinda, and trimmed on a Polar single-knife cutter.

Edited by Matthew Tierney
Designed by Crystal Sikma

Coach House Books
80 bpNichol Lane
Toronto ON M5S 3J4
Canada

416 979 2217
800 367 6360

mail@chbooks.com
www.chbooks.com